# Awesome Hamster Facts

## for Awesome Kids!

Belongs to:

‑ ‑ ‑ ‑ ‑ ‑ ‑ ‑ ‑ ‑ ‑ ‑ ‑ ‑ ‑ ‑ ‑ ‑ ‑ ‑

Howdy!

Hamsters first arrived in the United States in 1936. I wonder if they packed their cheeks?

Hamsters come in all shapes and sizes! The biggest grow to 13 inches and the smallest are only 2 to 4 inches long.

The Syrian hamster is the most popular. It's sometimes called the teddy bear hamster. Can you see why?

Hamsters need lots of exercise, that's why they love hamster wheels.

Hamsters LOVE to burrow and dig. In the wild their burrows keep them cool.

Hamsters are popular pets because they are gentle and easy to care for.

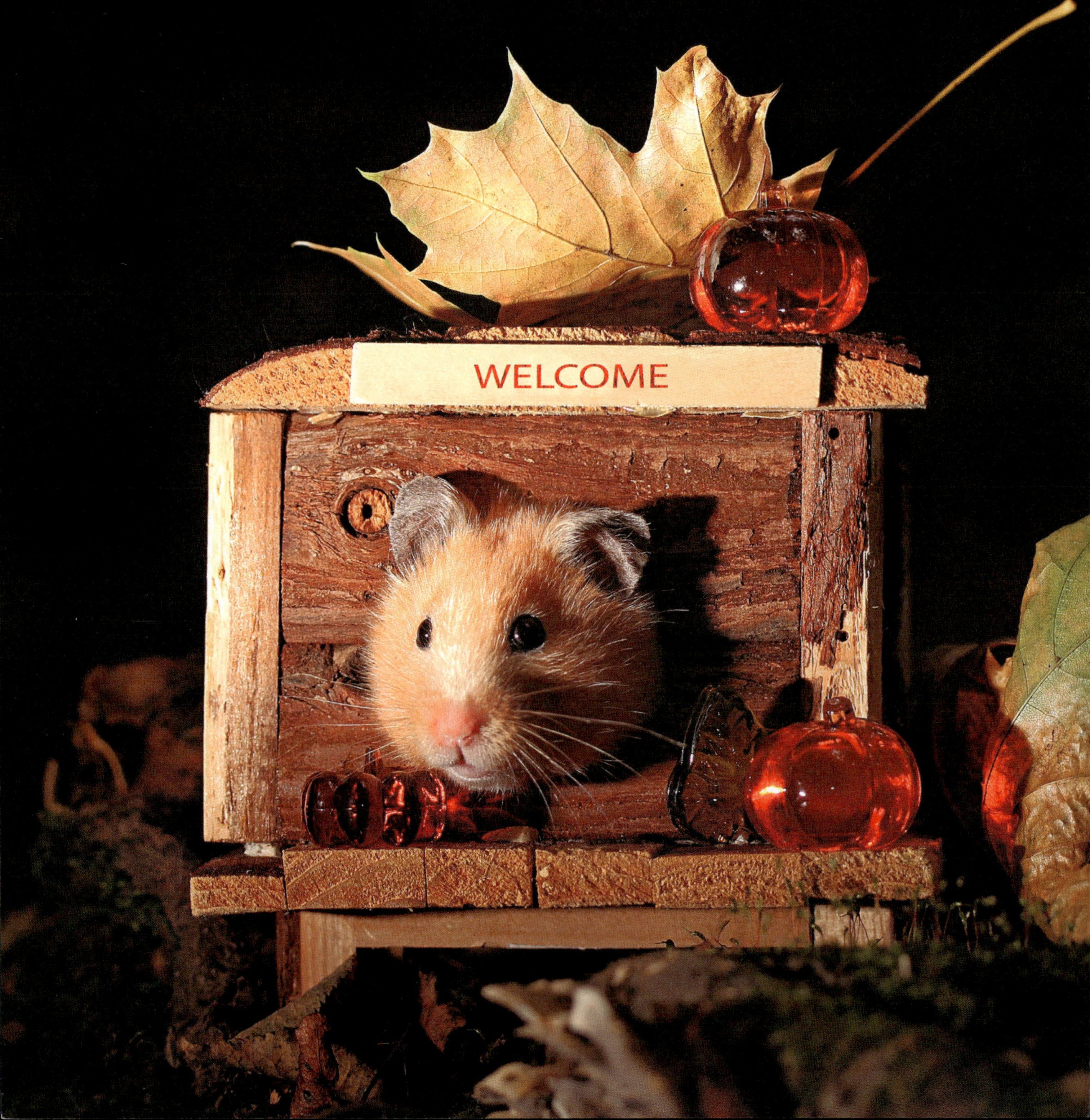
WELCOME

Hamsters stay awake at night and like to sleep during the day. This is called nocturnal.

Hamsters have very different personalities. Some like to be with other hamsters but some prefer to be alone.

Hamsters hide their food for later. You might see some under the bedding in a hamster cage. He'll get to it later!

Hamsters don't have good eyes. They get around using their backs which they rub on objects so they they can smell their way home!

Hamsters have pouches in their cheeks where they store food. It looks so cute!

Hamsters are popular pets because they are gentle and easy to care for.

Wild hamsters sometimes eat lizards and frogs. Gross!

Hamsters are just

AWESOME!

Printed in Great Britain
by Amazon